BLOOM UNDER MOONLIGHT

ALSO BY ANNIE SOPHIE LE

The Absence of You

BLOOM UNDER MOONLIGHT

ANNIE SOPHIE LE

ISBN: 978-1-7775696-2-4

CONTENTS

Burn, Burn, Burn   1
My Weather Girl   2
Unfettered   3
Grow to Spite Him   4
My Dear   6
Fire in Our Blood   7
Metamorphosis   8
Hope for the Hopeless   9
Medusa   10
Flower in the Concrete Jungle   11
Peony   12
The Mirror is Not Reality   14
Soulful   15
Swallowtail   16
Scar Tissue   17
Season   18
Strong   19
You Are No Less Than Me   20
Wildness   22
Lustful Moonlight   23
Satin Sheets   24
Today Is the Last Day I'll Think of You   25
Enough   27
Fire   28
A Poem for Lost Lovers   29
Tumble   30
Your Savage Heart   31
Past   32
She Exists for Herself   33
You Are Complete   36
The Taste of Freedom   37
Ashes   38
Healing Times   39

Funeral   40

Starry Smiles   41

Molting   42

Honeysuckle   43

Present   44

Firestorm Hearts   45

Shipwrecked   46

Love Letter   47

Blooming in the Dead of Winter   48

You Are Not Broken   49

She Doesn't Owe You Anything   50

Salt and Milk   51

The Grace of Sadness   53

In the Space Between Giving Up and Thriving   54

Welded   55

In Bloom   56

What Does Happiness Mean?   57

Whole   58

Create Yourself   59

For the Peony Girl   60

You Are Fire and Strength   61

Be Selfish with Yourself   62

Drown Them   63

Today   65

You Are Not Damaged   66

Who You Are Now   67

Peace   68

So Much More   69

Shameless   70

Invisible Made Visible   71

Overcome   72

Heal   73

Self-Titled   74

Lovely   75

Absent No Longer   76

Always and All Ways   77

Here   78

Hell   79

Survivor   80

Salt   81
Ouroboros   82
You Want to Be Okay Now   83
No Longer Absent   84
Rebellion   85
Wild Thing   86
Be at Peace   87
Living Presently   88
Remember   89
Waking Up   90
A Gut of Flowers   92
To Your Past Self   93
Graceful Heart   94
Victorious   95
Make Them Burn   97
Taste of Freedom   98
You Are Here   99
Warrior   100
Barbed Tongue   101
Persephone   102
Coming Home   103

Acknowledgments   105

BLOOM UNDER MOONLIGHT

BURN, BURN, BURN

Into the fire we are born,

stained and burned

but alive.

MY WEATHER GIRL

She was a torrential storm,
a drizzle turned deadly—
a hurricane.

I was a landslide,

dragged

away

by

h e r.

UNFETTERED

You are bound together
by infinite grace and strength,
birthed from a supernova.
They could only dream
of caging a wild bird.

GROW TO SPITE HIM

She speaks
but fears the sound of her voice,
and although she hurts,
she apologizes for speaking her mind.

She tells herself she is being irrational
for feeling this way, overreacting
and making a big deal
out of a grain of salt.

He knows this and plucks the words
she wants to hear from the air,
daisy petals tumbling from his mouth.

It is a game he plays, texting her
when speaking to her is too much effort.
Gaslighting her when she
is close to the truth
that she deserves better than him.

She spends her days breaking her limbs
to try to fit into the palms of his hands,

denying herself a chance to grow,
too afraid to be a lonely wildflower
among the weeds.

MY DEAR

you are not what happened to you

FIRE IN OUR BLOOD

Our strength
is immeasurable and unfathomable.
They will never know how deep
it lies.

It is in our decisions to cry
and it is in our hands that wipe away
the wetness below our eyes.
It is in us after the storm has ebbed
and in our constant momentum forward.

Even though we might be directionless,
our strength lies beneath
our soft flesh and glass smiles.

Our bones are made of steel and
there is fire in our blood.
In this,
we are strong.

METAMORPHOSIS

As the seasons change,
even dead things
grow and bloom.

HOPE FOR THE HOPELESS

Have hope
in these trying times.
Let your electric blood
thunder in the night sky
because you are strong,
and silence only
runs in the veins
of dead men.

MEDUSA

She repeats the words that she doesn't need him,
excising herself from him.
He took so much of her and left so little behind.
She is alone with herself; she is alone with him.

She burns, ignites when approached by men—
the type of men that take too much
and leave only bones behind.

But she has snakes for hair and an avalanche
for a tongue, and as they try to tame her,
she turns them to stone.

FLOWER IN THE CONCRETE JUNGLE

You are a dandelion
peeking through the cracks
in the concrete.

Others don't see your beauty,
thinking you a nuisance,
a weed to pluck and discard,

but you are resilient,
growing in the barren
jungle of hardness
and in the absence of warmth.

Despite the hardness
surrounding you,
you grew and bloomed,
surviving and enduring
where others wilted.

PEONY

You compare yourself to others,
finding faults where there are none.
You pick yourself apart,
rendering yourself into pieces,
wondering why you aren't whole.

You think you aren't enough,
seeing yourself as ugly,
and try to find your worth
in other people's faces.

But you don't see your beauty
in the quiet moments of your being,
or the way your eyes light up
when you speak about your passions,
or the smile that tugs at your lips
when you laugh at a joke.

You don't see the kindness
in your giving hands
or hear the sweetness in your words
when you are with friends.
You are beautiful in the quiet moments.

If only you could see yourself as others do,
then you would realize
you have been enough all along.

THE MIRROR IS NOT REALITY

your perception of yourself
is not how they see you

SOULFUL

The crow outside her window watches raptly
as her hips dance to music only her wild ears hear.
She laughs too loudly and smiles too widely,
this lively creature with sparkling eyes.

She is careless around others,
unhinged and free to be herself,
a crashing tidal wave against
the shore of crumbling sandcastles.

She is not beautiful because of her body.
She is beautiful because of her soul.

SWALLOWTAIL

You are not defeated.
Every day moves forward.
The day before
now rests in the past.

There needs to be an ending
to have a new beginning.
Hydrangeas wither away
in the winter but regrow
greater and fuller in the summer.

As they regrow, so must we—
even if it hurts,
even if we're scared.

We must shed our skins today
so we can begin again tomorrow.

SCAR TISSUE

If it hurts, it will heal—
or,
at least,
stop hurting so sharply.
Scar tissue is tougher
than untried flesh.

SEASON

There is grace
in her becoming—
peace in knowing that today
may not be the day she blooms—
but she will bloom.

The darkness doesn't scare her,
not anymore,
not since she became the moon,
the stars guiding her home,
guiding her to where she is meant to be.

And the space she inhabits
is filled with dreams
of mending her broken heart,
and this—
this is the season for healing.

STRONG

We have sewn our hearts
onto our sleeves, letting the world see
all that we hold dear.

This does not make us weak.
Our strength is in our grace
of feeling intensely and loving earnestly.

Sometimes we are vulnerable and fragile,
and they think we easily chip and break,
that we're porcelain falling to the ground,
shattering into millions of shards.

We're not afraid to carry
our hearts on our sleeves.
Let the world think we are weak
because we are soft.

We can be fragile and soft,
but it is their mistake
for believing this is our weakness,
when it is our strength.

YOU ARE NO LESS THAN ME

Your struggles
weigh the same as mine.
We are equal here,
for you stand beside me.

We are not comparable.
There are no numbers
tattooed on our eyelids,
making one of us
more worthy.

I am no less than you,
for our trophies
are both cast in gold.

We have won marathons
in mute soliloquies of sadness
and twisted fingers
that wove stories
in the air above our heads.

There is gold in our bones.

We have survived, you and I.
In our survival,
we are the same.

WILDNESS

This woman—
this beautiful creature
with a soul too bright for my eyes
and a smile
sweeter than honeysuckles—
lures me in, lures me deeper,
luring, luring, luring.

And I want to find out
everything about her,
understand all of her parts
and how she is built.

But she is too feral—
uncaged and unburdened—
and for me to love her,
I would have to capture her,
and I could only ever dream
of taming a wild bird.

LUSTFUL MOONLIGHT

Stars burning the skin
of the blanketed night—
punctuated, punctured.
Silence knitted into the skin
of the slumberous.
Not even the owls dare
break the moon's performance.

SATIN SHEETS

The morning he left, sneaking out of her bed,
quietly as the mice scurrying in the walls,
she awoke, cradled by empty silence,
disappointment pulsing against the rising sun.
She only wanted to wake up against his warm body,
covered in kissed declarations of their love.
Instead, she traces patterns in the empty space
on the wrinkled sheets he left behind.

TODAY IS THE LAST DAY I'LL THINK OF YOU

Every day begins with
I'm not going to think about you,
but ends with a soaked pillow
and a whispered confession:
Day forty-five without you.

You mark their vacancy
on a calendar in your head,
ticking every passing day—
wondering, hoping,
if there will come a day
when it will no longer be
you missing them
but a day celebrating you and your life—
letting go of the missing
and filling the hole they left behind
with smiles and laughter.

It comes slowly,
sneaking up on you
the way grief sneaks up on the living,
but instead of hurting,
there is numbness,

and in the numbness,
there is freedom.

You will greet the mornings quietly,
your head no longer filled with memories,
and when the evening begins,
your pillow will be dry—
a cloud of victory.

You won't think of them,
and every day won't be a day without them
but a day with you, fully present.
The nights won't be punctuated with
Day fifty-six without you.
Day seventy-eight without you.

You will realize
there will be survival without them.
You can survive—
despite their attempts
to break your heart—
you will let go of them
and you will thrive.

ENOUGH

I want to tell her
she can be happy with herself,
that it's okay to be alone.

She doesn't need
to follow him around
and bask in the little attention
he gives her.

If only she could see
her worth in herself
and not go looking
for it in someone else.

FIRE

The fire in your veins
isn't burning out,
and even when you're lost,
you will find yourself
where you were meant to be
all along.

A POEM FOR LOST LOVERS

The sound of rain
in the middle of the night
keeps her awake,
and she knots her limbs
around a blanket cast aside.

She reaches over
but finds only empty space—
void of him, void of them.

And in the silence of midnight,
she lets the tears fall,
promising herself
that tomorrow—
tomorrow she will thrive
without him.

TUMBLE

If you are afraid, remind yourself
that we're all afraid of the dark
until we learn
that the monsters are in our heads,
and for there to be light,
there must be darkness.

If you try and think you've failed,
redefine failure, and you'll see,
your victory is in your trying.

We all must stumble and trip,
fall down and tumble,
before we can run.

YOUR SAVAGE HEART

You are trying in these trying times,
and in the space between
a tidal wave and a sea of sunflowers,
you flourish, too bright for their eyes.

Even if they tried,
they could never clutch you in their hands.
You are a diamond, growing
from the hardness around you.
You are beautiful and intelligent,
valid and important.

They can't see what you've endured
or understand who you are,
for they are rainstorms
that dream of being hurricanes.

PAST

It is who you were

*(through circumstances,
through trauma and pain,
and mistakes made
and lessons learned)*

not who you are.

SHE EXISTS FOR HERSELF

He wishes he could decipher
her strange language of living.
She is a wild thing
who dances in moon dust
and exhales stars.

She is a woman
who is free to be herself—
damn everyone else.
A woman who doesn't care
what others think
and only lives
by the rules in her head.

He tried to hold her down,
attempted to stick pins
in her limbs into Styrofoam
to frame and display on his wall.

He loved her
in his own way of trying to tame
the wildness of her heart,
the kind of love

that wants to capture mermaids
for their beauty.

And she loved him
in her own way of loving from afar
but knowing
it's only a matter of time
before she leaves again.

Their love is beautiful
but gruesome and cruel,
and it comes in waves.
Some days are sour,
and other days sweet.

He emptied his guts
to make room for her,
but she wouldn't build
a home in him.
It wasn't in her to make a home
in anyone but herself.

She wishes she could understand
this need to be free,
but she's always been on the run,
and love won't change that.

Their love turned to poison—
he was bitter he couldn't tame her,
and she was resentful
that he would try.

So he replaced her
with someone else,
someone that wanted
the neat package

of settling down, settling for less.
Someone that wanted
to be hung over the mantelpiece
and be worshipped.

She was a star—
burning too brightly,
scalding the hands of those
who tried to capture her.

He let her go,
but there are days
when he wonders
what could've been.

He still thinks about her—
her unruly hair
that was never combed
and her crooked smile
that came easily and left too swiftly,

and it is only in his memories
that he can capture her
and trap her in his head.

YOU ARE COMPLETE

You are strong without him.
You are worthy when alone.
You can love yourself,
despite him not loving you.
You do not need him
to be whole.

THE TASTE OF FREEDOM

Beautifully heartbroken,
she found herself
in losing you.

ASHES

You are fire,
so burn the world to ash
until nothing remains
but you.

HEALING TIMES

Forgotten are the slow winter days—
days when the countertop was covered with mugs
stained with long-forgotten stale coffee,
too depressed to clean, unable to move,
other than to breathe.

Now the world is no longer
monochromatic greys of getting by,
but is filled with the watercolour intensity of life.
The winter of melancholy is a memory now.

There is promise here—
promise of laughter and hope uncovered,
and the quiet triumph of wars won
and healing times ahead.

FUNERAL

She is stuck under his fingernails,
a sliver embedded in his skin.
He is a scab on her arm
that she picks and picks.
There won't be healing for them,
no closure or forgiveness.
And the yawning gap
between their fingers
becomes a burial ground
for everything they once shared.

STARRY SMILES

They tried to capture you,
but you flew
from their grasps
under the kiss of moonlight.
Despite their best attempts
at breaking you,
you blossomed
into a beautiful wild thing
and made a home
among the stars.

MOLTING

Your past
does not define you
or confine you
to live a certain way.
You are free to change,
to make your own decisions
and be whoever you want to be.

HONEYSUCKLE

I write poems
made from honeysuckles
dedicated to your beauty.

I weave daisies
from these inky shapes
into a crown
to place upon your head.

You are the queen of summer
with your wild heart
and eyes carved from stars.

And wherever you go,
sunflowers bloom.

PRESENT

You are free—
here and now,
you are free.

FIRESTORM HEARTS

There is gold in our bones
and thunder in our hearts.

Every time we sleep,
fireworks and symphonies
fill our dreams.

We dig our heels into the ground
against the tornado of trying times.

We are strong
and we will overcome.

SHIPWRECKED

This is the season for healing,
for a journey of self-discovery,
and when we find ourselves,
we'll hang our skin
in a gallery for all to admire,
triumphant and proud—
proud that we found ourselves
when we had been lost at sea.

LOVE LETTER

I hope
you find your way
out of this.

BLOOMING IN THE DEAD OF WINTER

When everything is sleeping
beneath a blanket of white ash,
you will find your voice.
It will give you strength
when you realize
that within you,
there is a garden
where your bravery
grows.

YOU ARE NOT BROKEN

Despite their attempts at breaking you,
you are bound together
by enduring strength
that will carry you through storms,
even when you think
your feet will fail you.

SHE DOESN'T OWE YOU ANYTHING

She matters, even if she isn't your

sister,
daughter,
wife,
or child.

She matters because she is her own person.

SALT AND MILK

In the waves of who she was
and who she wanted to be,
she found herself
in the spilling of her salt.

With the loudness of the silence—
too still in its quiet,
she stood taller than her shadow,
unwavering in her determination
that she will not fall this time.

She will not be consumed
by three-worded cages
of *I Love You* and *I Hate You*.

She is free to grow into a violet,
to be herself, to be the moon,
to be, to be, to be.

She will not allow herself
to fall for someone smaller than she is.
As if she could love anyone

more than she loves herself.
As if she would cry over spilt milk.

THE GRACE OF SADNESS

Sometimes there aren't lessons to be learned
in falling apart and imploding inwards.
Sometimes you just need to be
and rest in the grace of being sad.

IN THE SPACE BETWEEN GIVING UP
AND THRIVING

Against the pressure
of giving up or moving on,
throbbing and thudding
against your skin—
a dull ache you think
you can no longer bear,
tiny threads and cracks form
along your body,
and you feel as though
if it were not for your skin,
you would come apart
in a bursting shower of hail.
But in the spaces
between the cracks,
your light shines through.

WELDED

Remember,
you are steel
forged in fire.

IN BLOOM

I could write poems
about how beautiful her soul is.
I could dedicate these inky shapes
to the kindness in her smiles
and her giving heart on her sleeve.

I often worry the hardness
of the world will cut into
her milk-fleshed skin,
soft as peony petals.

I want to wrap her in a cocoon
of velvet and keep her away
from the concrete jungle.

But I am foolish to mistake
her softness for weakness,
for she is stronger than steel.

Despite the hurt she endured
and the calluses on her fingers,
she blooms like a wildflower
beneath the sun.

WHAT DOES HAPPINESS MEAN?

You'll have to let go of the notion
that you are your illness.
Stop reducing yourself
to the name of your diagnosis,
to nothing more than a mess.

For once,
you want to move on and let go—
let go of everything you were.
But who will you be
when you get better?

There is a balance between
the ephemeral mania-induced happiness
and true visceral happiness.
And you are slowly learning the difference,
so slowly you don't even notice at first.

You taste happiness, and you realize,
you are happy—
not because you are no longer sad,
but because you still have your sad days
and you are learning to appreciate them both.

WHOLE

You are the sum
of rainstorms
that trailed over you
and tornadoes devouring
all in their wake.

CREATE YOURSELF

you don't have to live by their rules anymore

FOR THE PEONY GIRL

There is this girl with wide green eyes
and needlepoint-straight hair
that she curls into brown waves.

When she smiles,
the moon silences in the night sky.
Even the stars are in awe
of her beautiful soul
and the kindness of her hands.

She is as soft as a peony,
but don't mistake her softness
for a weakness.

She is stronger than steel
and when she shines,
she shines brighter
than a supernova.

YOU ARE FIRE AND STRENGTH

You are proud of the scars you bear
and hurricanes weathered.
When you think you can't
survive another storm,
you will find yourself
stronger than before,
a wildflower blooming
during a drought.

BE SELFISH WITH YOURSELF

self-care is self-preservation

DROWN THEM

They take away your dignity
and are unwilling to see
everything you have endured.

It is yet another way for them
to disregard your humanity
and negate your struggles.

Who are they to tell you
how to deal with your hurt?
Who are they to decide
what is best for you?

They say:
It's in the past.
Get over it.
Move on.
Learn to let things go.

So you remain bitter and angry—
at those who hurt you,
at those who invalidate you.

Their cruel words reopen
the sore wound
you've tried so hard to heal.
Let the anger take root,
and use it as your armour.

TODAY

bloom where you are

YOU ARE NOT DAMAGED

Every:

lick of fire you've endured
staining fingerprint left behind
memory that trails after you
hurt and teardrop

has made you into who you are.

You are weathered and strong,
for you are still here,
and that is all that matters.

WHO YOU ARE NOW

You are impenetrable steel,
forged and hammered.
Whenever you feel
your skin cracking
and you might shatter,
coming apart,
remember,
you were born from fire.

PEACE

Plant seeds in a garden,
so when you escape
the hurricane,
you will have a home
among the wildflowers.

SO MUCH MORE

Your worth
is more than your productivity and success.

Your worth
is not property or money.
It cannot be easily measured or defined.

Your worth
is what you survived and who you are.

SHAMELESS

The shame you carry
from what they did to you
is not yours to bear.

You are not their shame.

INVISIBLE MADE VISIBLE

Maybe if your resilience
was visible for all to see,
then they'd acknowledge
and appreciate your efforts
of enduring and surviving.

OVERCOME

Even if you falter,
you will survive this.

HEAL

The journey to healing
isn't a one-way street.

It isn't linear nor tidy.

It is messy,
but it is yours.

SELF-TITLED

This is your life.

Don't write yourself out of it.

LOVELY

Even after they have gone,
you carry them with you,
building a flowerbed of dead things
to blossom into sunflowers
that smile and bloom
when you are near,
reminding you
that the love they once gave you
can still make beautiful things.

ABSENT NO LONGER

Recognize
the strength it took
for you to be here.

Even though
you wanted to give up
and disappear,
you are here.

ALWAYS AND ALL WAYS

You are sad and tired,
not defeated.

You are not broken
but mending with every passing day.

And when you wake from this fog,
you will be unconquerable,
stronger than before.

With an unshakable heart
and the certainty
that when the next storm hits,
you will face it.

You will survive it,
even if you falter,
you will survive.

HERE

your voice is powerful

you are enough

you are independent

you are strong

you are alive in the space you take up

HELL

the only way to get over it
is to go through it

SURVIVOR

Sometimes,
a step forward
is a step backward.
But tell yourself,
you can survive this
because you have survived
much worse.

SALT

Anger doesn't taste bitter or sweet—
it is colourless and unbiased.

It fills your veins with fire,
burning your face.

Let it be,
this anger of yours.

Give it
space to breathe
and grow.

OUROBOROS

it always begins and ends with love

YOU WANT TO BE OKAY NOW

So many people have moved on
and left you behind,
replacing you in their lives.
You have been missing for too long,
but not anymore.

You will get better.
It won't be sudden
but it will happen
because you have survived.

You survived and endured,
through hell and back
and back again.

And now,
now you can heal and live.

NO LONGER ABSENT

How different it feels
to be present
in your own life.

REBELLION

Be defiantly happy.

WILD THING

She holds the glowing moon—
a pearl—
in her open palms
and coos sweet lullabies
to the night.

The silence
wraps around her,
settling in her soul.
She is quiet,
thankful to be alive.

She is alone in the night,
but she is never lonely,
not with the moonlight
and constellations
keeping her company.

BE AT PEACE

Vacillating between
getting by or falling backward,
wondering whether
to tumble or hold steady.

The answers won't come today—
or the day after that—
so rest your head and know
you're doing your best.

LIVING PRESENTLY

We crawled through the mud
to get here.
We walked across simmering coals
to let go of our traumas and hurt.
There were hurricanes survived
and tornadoes endured,
and now,
in these trying times,
we cup our hearts in our palms
and thrive,
coming alive
in the space we take up.

REMEMBER

you are not defined by your illness

WAKING UP

You suddenly grow tired
of being tired.
You don't want to be okay
with not being okay—
not anymore.

Now you want to be okay,
to be fine with yourself and your life.
You want to move on from this,
move on to better things.
The thought terrifies you—
it's foreign and unreal.

You find yourself staring
at your reflection, not knowing
who is staring back at you.
When did you become faceless?

Then there is the fear of losing yourself.
Who are you, outside of your illness?
You've spent your entire life
around the melancholic campfire,
making a home in your brokenness.

So what do you do?
Do you remain the same
and be okay with being miserable?
Or do you become tired with being blue
and want to be content now?

Instead of surviving and enduring,
you want to live and thrive.

A GUT OF FLOWERS

If only they could see everything
you have been through.
Then they would be in awe
of the petals that grow
from your chest
and of the ease
with which you smile.

TO YOUR PAST SELF

You fought so hard
and did your best.
Don't blame yourself
for the choices you made
with what little you had.
But you don't have to fight anymore.
You can rest and let go.
Your present self will carry you.

GRACEFUL HEART

She holds onto hope—
not for miracles or answers,

but for the certainty that she will know
peace in the unknowns.

Just as she carries strength,
she will carry herself

through the wildness
with grace.

VICTORIOUS

We live in concrete jungles,
bitter shapes of metal bones
and glass hearts.

We are survivors,
weary shoulders hunched
against the storms
of these trying times.

We find peace in our anger,
strength in our veins,
we are free and wild,
we are steel.

We are victorious in our survival.
Our battle cries are louder
than the crashing waves.

We hold hope
in the palms of our hands.
We are strong and unshackled.
We are unfettered.
We are stone.

There are cosmos in our veins
and happiness in our lungs.

We are free now,
and with brave hearts
and courageous bodies,
we are unconquerable.

MAKE THEM BURN

You are a kaleidoscope
of stained glass framed in gold,
and when the sun
shines down on you,
you are blinding in your beauty.

TASTE OF FREEDOM

We are not disposable—
even if our sadness says otherwise.

We are not worthless—
even if our self-loathing
whispers differently.

We are more than our darkness.
We are never going back.
We are not who we were.

The past holds no sway over us—
not anymore.

So we move forward
and set ourselves on fire.

We are free,
we are free,
we are free.

YOU ARE HERE

Even if it doesn't feel like it,
here,
in the space you take up,
you are coming alive.
It is deserved,
and it is worthy.

You are meant to be.

WARRIOR

Wilted and weary,
she closes her eyes
against the moon,
and when the sun rises,
so will she,
stronger
than she was
the day before.

BARBED TONGUE

Speak your truth—
even if it hurts,
even if you are scared.

It is yours,
and only when releasing it
will you find freedom.

PERSEPHONE

In the winter,
when everything is sleeping
under a blanket of white embers,

she will find her voice
among the snowflakes that tumble
from the sky and the icicles
hanging above her head.

She will realize,
despite her darkness,
her heart was always in bloom.

COMING HOME

You are alive,
you are here,
you are home.

ACKNOWLEDGMENTS

Thank you Misti Wolanski and Anne Kopas, for your talent and thoughtfulness in helping me polish off this collection. I couldn't have done it without you.

Bố, thank you—as always, for believing in me when I didn't believe in myself, for being my cheerleader and my lighthouse guiding me home. I love you.

Thank you to my friends for your unwavering presences in my life. Thank you for the laughter and the smiles, the inspiration, and the love. I love you.

Thank you, dear reader, for being here with me in these words and in this collection you hold in your hands. You have survived so much and been through hell. I hope you know how strong you can be and how graceful you are. Take care of yourself.

Live and thrive,
Annie Sophie Le

www.anniesophiele.com
Instagram: @anniesophiele